purposes and should thus be thought of as universal. As befitting its nature, it is presented without assurance regarding its prolonged validity or interim quality. Trademarks that are mentioned are done without written consent and can in no way be considered an endorsement from the trademark holder.

Table of Contents

Introduction

The world that we live in now is full of things, of material possessions. We are bombarded with advertisements all of the time, ones telling us that we need to have this item or that item. It is a way for big companies to make a lot of money, and they promise us it will help make us happy, help us make friends, and help us have a better life.

In reality, none of this is true. Most of us spend more and more money on material possessions and find out that it leaves us feeling empty inside. It takes up a lot of our time as we work more to purchase more items, we clean up more to get those items out of our way, and we assign too much power and emotions to those items because they are all we are connected to. This can lead to a real problem that many people don't even know that they are dealing with.

When you decide that it is time to declutter, you will start making some drastic changes to your life. Minimalism is an idea that hasn't caught on yet too much of the modern world, but the idea that you can actually be happy, that you can slow down in life, and really enjoy things and feel less stress, is very comforting and positive to a lot of people. And the process of decluttering different parts of your life can really help to make this a reality.

This guidebook is going to talk a bit more about decluttering and all the benefits that come with it. We start out with an explanation of minimalism, and how it can be a great way to help you live your life to the fullest. Minimalism is different for everyone, and despite popular belief, it doesn't mean that you need to get rid of everything that you own. Minimalism can mean different things to each person, as long as you make intentional decisions about things you purchase and only go for the ones that actually make you happy.

After talking about minimalism, we will spend some time looking into decluttering. We will look at some of the benefits of doing this in your home, some of the reasons that people have yet to start with decluttering, and the importance of managing your time and setting up a routine to keep the decluttering process going.

This all leads up to some practical steps that you can take to clean up every room in your home. We will take a look at how to clean the kitchen, the bathrooms, the bedrooms, the living rooms, the office, your garage and basement, and even those messy closets. While you should take this process slowly to help prevent yourself from becoming overwhelmed, by the time you are done with this guidebook, you are going to see a vast improvement in the cleanliness of your home, in the amount of clutter that is present, and the amount of freed and stress that you feel in your life.

We will then end with some of the different decluttering methods that you can use, including some that have become very popular, and can help you get the most out of your decluttering session.

Many people avoid decluttering their lives because they are worried about how long it will take, they add too much value to the items they own, or they just don't want to handle it at all. With the help of this guidebook, you will be able to declutter your home and finally find the peace and stress relief that you have been looking for.

Chapter 1:
What is Minimalism?

B efore we get started with the idea of decluttering, it is important to understand minimalism and how it can come into play. It is actually quite simple. It is the idea that you live with as little as possible. Instead of getting involved in a culture that is all about purchasing more things, and trying to keep up with your neighbors, and purchase more materials goods. While many people hear the word minimalism and assume it means they can't have a home, or a car, and never travel or do anything, and only one a handful of items, this is kind of to the extreme. Minimalism doesn't mean you have to live in a hole and have nothing. It just means that you learn what you really need to survive, without all the extra stuff that just takes up space.

Minimalism is a tool that is going to assist you in finding freedom that you could never imagine. It can provide you with some freedom from fear, worry, from being overwhelmed, and even from guilt and depression. Even better, it can help you gain some freedom from the trappings of the consumer culture, that most people have built their lives around.

This doesn't mean that there is something really bad about owning material possessions. If you actually use those items and find real enjoyment from them, then they are great. But the problem comes when we give too much meaning to the things that we own, giving so much attention to these things than our personal growth, our passions, our relationships, and our health. It becomes a problem when we have things just to have them there, without having them actually do anything for you.

It is fine to own a home, raise a family, and have material possessions when you are a minimalist. This is not about getting rid of everything. But it is a method that helps you to make these decisions, decisions about what you purchase and own, in a more deliberate and conscious manner.

There are lots of people who are successful with being a minimalist who are able to lead an appreciably different life. There are different types of minimalists who do well. Some like to keep themselves down to just a few possessions and nothing else, mainly to make life simpler and to keep them away from materialistic thoughts. But there are plenty of these minimalists who have cars, homes, families, careers, and more, they simply just learn how to make smart and deliberate decisions about material objects before they make a purchase.

The next question that you may have is how people can be so different and still be considered minimalists. This can bring us back to the first question that we asked — "What is minimalism?" This can be complicated to describe, but to keep it simple, minimalism is a tool that can help you get rid of the excesses in life in favor of focusing on what is important so you can find freedom, fulfillment, and happiness.

There are a lot of things that minimalism is able to help you out with many different things including:

- Helps you grow as an individual

- Focus more on your health

- Create more and consume less

- Experience some real freedom

- Discover the mission that you should really have in life.

- Pursue your passions

- Live in the moment rather than focusing on the future or the past so much

- Reclaim some of our time since you don't have to worry about cleaning nonstop.

- Eliminate some of the discontents on our lives

- Discover your purpose in life

- Rid your life of all the extra stuff that is just in the way

- Be able to contribute to the world beyond ourselves

When you learn how to incorporate minimalism into your life, even just a little bit, it provides you with a way to find lasting happiness, and this is what everyone is really looking for. We all want to be happy. But while other people focus on finding happiness through the different things that they own, a minimalist is going to search for happiness through their life and the memories they make. This means that you get the benefit of choosing what is necessary, and what is superfluous in your own life.

Minimalism has the possibility to be different for every person. Some people will use it as a way to help them keep their life in order and actually enjoy things. But for some people, a good life includes lots of books so they will make sure they have a large library around them. Some people like to take trips with their families and will use their money towards that. Just because you have a few things in your life and you don't live like a monk to be considered a minimalist in your life.

A few things to consider when it comes to figuring out what minimalism is and how you can bring it into your life include:

- **It is about intentionality**: Minimalism is marked with intentionality, purpose, and clarity. At the core, this idea is all about the intentional promotion of the things that we already value the most, and the removal of everything that will take our attention away from it. This type of life means that you need to be intentional with what you do so that you see marked improvements in all parts of your life.

- **It provides you with some freedom from the passion that you have to possess items**: Our modern culture has taught us that the only way that you can have a good life is when you accumulate more things. The more you own, the happier you will be. But this is a very false idea. This can actually trap us, making us value items too much, making us follow these items and what is the latest trend, and dealing with all the debt that comes with this. Minimalism is going to bring you some freedom from the all-consuming passion that most people have to possess more items. This lifestyle is going to let us step off the treadmill of consumerism, and helps you to seek more happiness in other places. You can then start to value your self-care, the experiences you have, and your relationships.

- **It offers you some freedom from many modern manias**: Our modern world moves at a feverish pace. We always rush around and feel stressed, we work long hours to pay the bills, and still fall more into debt. We are always running around and being busy, but we can't form good relationships, or ever relax and enjoy the things that we have. Minimalism is great because it helps us to slow down our lives and reduce some of the stress that we feel. We get the freedom to disengage, it allows us to get rid of anything that is frivolous, and can make it easier to just find endeavors that add some value to our lives.

- **It offers freedom from duplicity**: Although no one really chooses it, most people live in duplicity. They live one life around their neighbors, one around their co-workers, and one around their family. This is due to the lifestyle that they choose. But with minimalism, you are able to choose a life that is simple, one that is consistent and united. You can have the same kind of lifestyle no matter who you are around, and this can make things so much easier.

- **It is counter-cultural**: Right now, we are in a world that idolizes celebrities. Their lives are held up as the standard that everyone should live by. Those who have a minimalist life are not shown by the media, because they don't fit into the current consumerist culture that politicians and corporations try to promote. While most people are going for fame, success, and more possessions, minimalism is going to ask you to slow down, consume more, but still enjoy your life more. And after following this kind of lifestyle for just a short amount of time, it is easy to see that we have made the right decision and that this method is way better compared to the way we did before.

- **Minimalism is more internal**: Minimalism is more a matter of the heart than anything else. After all that clutter externally has been removed, minimalism has the space to address the way that we live our lives and enjoy our relationships. And in some cases, those outside of our family may not even recognize that we have taken on this kind of lifestyle. But if you learn how to declutter, and only live with the things that you need and that make you truly happy, you are going to find your life can be quite different than before.

- **It is achievable**: Despite what our current culture may tell us, minimalism is achievable. We don't need to have the latest and greatest gadget. We don't need to fill our homes with a ton of things to make us happy. What we need is our family, or friends, and a few other things to help us have the happy life that we need. Minimalism can help you to reach that goal and reach the ultimate happiness that you want.

Minimalism is an idea that is a bit different from what our modern society tells us what is normal. While others are following the latest trend and trying to get as many possessions as possible, you could be living your best and happiest life simply by following the idea of minimalism.

Chapter 2:
What is a Decluttering Mindset?

B efore you get started on your method of decluttering, it is important to realize that this takes a certain type of mindset. If you are too attached to your items, or you start out feeling that you will only get rid of a few things, or that this is going to be too difficult to accomplish, then things are not going to go the way that you plan. Having a certain mindset ahead of time can make a big difference in how much you can accomplish. Some of the things that you should consider when you get started with your own decluttering and help you with a decluttering mindset include:

- **Make decisions quickly**: The longer you think about something, the more likely it is that you will keep that item in your home, even if you never use it. The first reaction that you have to an item should be the one that you go with. Give yourself 30 seconds or less on each item. Make the decision and don't look back.

- **Have a clear list of criteria that help you to make decisions**: Before you get started with decluttering, take some time to write out a list of the criteria you will follow, when you get rid of, or keep things. Then, as you go through each room, keep this list on hand. If the item doesn't meet your criteria, it is time to get rid of it.

- **Pick a day when you are ready**: If you have a stressful week at work, if you are feeling sick, or if you really don't feel doing any decluttering, it is fine to hold off starting or take a break along the way. Sometimes you may need to give yourself some time before you continue on in the process. Just take that break and get back to it as soon as possible. Enter into the process of decluttering with a can-do attitude and you will be able to get the work done.

- **Have limits on how much of the sentimental stuff can stick around**: Sentimental stuff is great, and it is fine to keep a few of them around. This is especially good if you actually use them in some manner in your home. For example, if you have a wall clock that your grandfather gave you and you still use it, then it is fine to keep it around. But there is a limit to how much of this sentimental stuff should stick around. Pick a number of how many you are comfortable with and then get rid of everything else.

- **Have a wait and see box**: There are going to be some items that you are not sure what you want to do with right that moment. You should try to make firm decisions with your stuff, deciding whether to keep or get rid of them right away. But there may be a few things that you are uncertain about. Instead of putting it back into your closet or back in the room, put it in your wait and see box. Then, if you don't use it within a few months, it is time to get rid of that item because you don't really need it.

- **Don't allow obligation or guilt with presents**: One issue that can come up when you get started with decluttering is guilt or a sense of obligation when someone gives you a gift. You don't want to feel inconsiderate if you get a present from someone and then you throw it away. But if you aren't even using the gift, and it is just taking up space in your home, then it really isn't being used in the manner the giver intended. Never hold onto a present just because someone you love gave it to you. If it doesn't bring you joy, you aren't using it, and it is just taking up space and cluttering up your home, then it doesn't matter who gave it to you, it is time to get rid of that item.

- **Have tunnel vision and stay in just one room at a time**: When you get started with decluttering a specific room, don't let yourself fall prey to a bunch of distractions. This can seem pretty simple to remember but there are times when you need to watch the kids, you think of something else that you need to get done that day, or you just can't seem to concentrate. But when you get started with decluttering a room, turn on the tunnel vision and just concentrate on getting that room done. That can help you to stay focused and get the work done faster than if you stop and go as you handle other tasks.

- **Don't overdo it. One room a day is fine**: Decluttering can take some time to accomplish. It is not a task that you can rush and while it can be done quickly, for the first time, you need to just focus your work on just one room at a time. Once you are done with one room, take it easy and do something else. This helps to take the stress out of the job and can help you to not get burnt out from the process.

- **Find easy ways to get rid of your stuff**: If you make it too difficult to get rid of the items that you have, then you are going to run into trouble. You will separate things out in your home, but then you won't actually get rid of them. These things will stay in your car, or in the closet, or somewhere else in your home and just causes a mess again. Find the method that works the best for you to get that stuff out of your home right away.

- **Maintain the clutter free zone in your home**: To prevent more things coming into your home and causing a mess, it is important to maintain an environment that is clutter free. To do this, make a list of all the things that you absolutely need to have in your home. Whether it is in household goods, appliances, clothes, or something else, know exactly what you need. Anything else is extra and shouldn't make it into your home. Don't waste time browsing through catalogs, going through stores, or looking online, because these are very good at convincing you to make a purchase of something that you don't need. Stick with the basics, the necessities, and you will be able to keep the clutter out of your home.

- **Make decluttering a habit**: Decluttering should not be something you do just once and then never pay attention to again. If you want to make sure that your home stays organized, then decluttering needs to become a regular part of your routine. Make it a habit to declutter once a week, or to get rid of something from your home each day. It is a simple way to keep your home clean and free of clutter.

A decluttering mindset can make a world of difference when it comes to how much stuff you can get rid of, and how clean you can keep your house. If you are too attached to the sentimental things, or if you are too overwhelmed with the work ahead, then you may burn out and not want to keep up with the work. Adopt some of the ideas above, and you will find that it is easier to keep up with decluttering and simplifying your life.

Chapter 3:
Top 10 Reasons Why You Haven't Started Decluttering Already

W hile decluttering may seem like the perfect solution to your messy house and messy life, there are still tons of people who don't do any sort of decluttering, or they do it on a very rare basis. There are many reasons why people may try to avoid decluttering their homes and lives, but often it has to do with finding too much sentimental value in things, and feeling overwhelmed at all the work that needs to be done with this process. Some of the top reasons why you, or someone else, may not have already started with decluttering their homes and lives may include:

1. **The memories**: It is pretty common for people to hold onto their favorite memories through objects, but this is also a reason why they are stuck in the past. Many times, the items that we hold onto are just reminders of a good time in our past or a period of our lives that we want to remember. Always trust that these experiences are going to stay in your heart. If you need to, take a picture of that item and then give the item away if you aren't using it.

2. **They aren't sure how long to keep things**: This can be a big issue in many homes. How do you know it is time to sell, donate, or toss an item if you have no idea how long to keep it in the first place. Some items should be gotten rid of earlier than others, but most of the time, we hold onto items for much longer than we need to.

3. **You don't know how to let go**: Letting go of items, especially ones that you feel are sentimental, can be a big part of the decluttering process. This can be hard when it comes to letting an item go or not. But you need to learn that these things are just things, and nothing that is important. It is fine to let them go and move on to bigger and better things in your life.

4. **A sense of security**: Certain objects can provide people with a false sense of security. We make ourselves feel like we are comfortable and secure when we acquire things. This could just be the way that the person is wired or it could be something that goes back to childhood.

When going through your home, ask yourself if you really need that item at all.

While you don't have to go through and overanalyze how things are, it is still a good idea to stop and think about why you purchase, store, and use things before deciding whether or not to keep that item.

5. **A remorse over a bad purchase**: It is common for people to make a purchase on a whim, and many times this can result in them overspending on the item, and then feeling guilty when the item sits in its original box without being used at all. After spending a lot of money on an item, it can be hard to face the feelings of failure for that bad decision.

It is fine to feel buyer's remorse sometimes, but this should not be an excuse to hold onto the item. Donate them to someone who may need them. Use this as a learning experience to keep yourself from doing the same things again.

6. **A fear of letting things go**: Another issue that some people may encounter is that they have a fear of letting things go. They may be so attached to their stuff for many different reasons that they are scared of letting it go. It may be a fear of scarcity or not having enough, which could create a habit of hoarding and stockpiling, or a fear that they will forget the memories, which is why some people may hold onto memorabilia, photos, and artwork.

The best thing that you can do to help this is to address the reasons why you hold onto things and then create a plan that allows you to let go of these things. You may find that it seems a bit silly when you actually say it out loud, and you may then be willing to let the item go.

7. **The idea of decluttering is too overwhelming**: For some people, the reason they don't spend time decluttering is that it is just too much for them to handle. They may feel that it is overwhelming to go through everything in their homes, and then making quick decisions about whether to keep that item or not. And the idea of doing the physical work to get rid of items can be hard. The best thing to do here is to remember that decluttering doesn't have to happen overnight. It is fine to take a week, a month, or even a few months to declutter your whole home. No one expects you to go through and declutter the whole house overnight.

8. **They don't know where to start**: Most people have larger homes, ones that can hold a lot of stuff, and it is sometimes hard to know where to start. They may walk into a room and wonder what they need to work on first. This can sometimes be bad enough that they then get overwhelmed, and start looking through things and not doing the work at hand.

9. **They don't realize how much clutter is actually in their home**: Some people may be in denial about how much of a mess they actually have in their homes. They may notice that there is a bit of a mess, but they say things like "I've been busy", "I have kids that make it messy", and so on. What they don't realize is that by decluttering and organizing things in their home, they could actually help to make life easier and require less cleaning.

10. **They don't want to put in the time or effort**: Some people are just too lazy to get the work done. We are all busy and have lots of activities to get to, but there are some people who look at the clutter and just sweep it under the rug. They don't want to deal with it and would rather spend their time doing something else. But with a little bit of time out of your day, you can make a big difference in how clean your home is and how much clutter is found there, saving you time and energy the next time you want to clean or you have trouble finding something you need.

There are many different reasons why people do not want to spend time cleaning up their homes and decluttering their lives. And the reasons above are some of the most common. If you find that you are suffering from some of the reasons above, it is time to make some changes and realize all the good that decluttering can do in your life.

Chapter 4:
Top 10 Benefits of Turning Your Decluttering Into a Habit

D ecluttering your home may seem like such a simple process, one that may make your home a bit cleaner, but that is about it. But there are so many benefits that you can get when it comes to decluttering your home. You can free up more of your time, spend less of your time and energy on cleaning the home, and it can even help you to improve your overall health.

Some of the benefits that you can enjoy when you pick up a decluttering habit include:

1. Keeps your home clean without having to waste the weekend

How many times have you gotten to the weekend, and dreaded it because you knew you would need to spend the whole time or at least a good chunk of it, cleaning up? Many people find that when there is a lot of clutter around the home, they end up spending way too much of their free time trying to keep it all clean and tidy.

If you go through the process of decluttering, you can help get rid of a lot of the stuff that is in your home. This can go a long way when it comes to how much you need to pick up during the weekends. If you are able to keep up on the decluttering during the week and make sure that you don't start going through and purchasing more stuff after the process is done, you will free up more of your weekend to do the things that you want.

For those who are tired of wasting all their free time on the weekends or day off, then decluttering may be the process that you need. It does take some time in the beginning, simply because there is so much clutter and not a lot of organization throughout your home. But once you get these things down, you are going to see a big difference in how quickly you can clean up the home. A few minutes each night should be plenty (once the major decluttering process is done) and you can then spend the rest of your free time doing what you want to do.

2.   Makes it easier to find what you need

Think about how much time you have wasted in your life trying to find the things that you need? It can be frustrating to look for the keys when it is time to go or to search around for another important thing that you need before starting your day. The more clutter you have, the harder it is to find the items you really need. When you go through the process of decluttering, you can get rid of all the extra and unnecessary things, freeing up more time and space for the things that are actually important. And overall, this will make it much easier for you to find what you need.

How many times have you had to scramble around in the morning to find your keys? How many times have you been frustrated because you couldn't find what you need? How many times have you been late to an appointment or an important meeting, because you spent that time searching for the right thing to wear, or for the document you needed to take with you?

Decluttering can make this whole process so much easier. You will learn that everything has a place, and you will get into the habit of placing them in those places. And when the clutter is gone, it is easier to look around a room and find exactly what you are looking for without all the hassle.

3.   Less time picking things up

Any time that you clean the house, you spend the majority of that time and effort picking up clutter. Most of the stuff is unnecessary and just in the way, and most of it is waste. You could spend hours cleaning up your home and most of it is stuff that only has the purpose of ending up back on your floor. If you get rid of that clutter, you can spend less time picking up your home and more time doing something that you enjoy.

If you get rid of half the items that are in your home, you could technically get rid of half the time that you usually spend with your cleaning process. The more that you can donate or throw out, the easier it can be for you to clean up the home, and then spend more time doing the things that you really want to do. Even if the process of decluttering your whole home may seem daunting and a little boring, think of all the free time you are going to gain later on.

4. It is easier to clean your home without all the clutter in your way

This may seem pretty obvious, but the less stuff you have in your home on the floor or on the counter, the faster you can clean up the home. If you are constantly putting the stuff away just to see it back on the floor, chances are you are dealing with a lot of clutter and it is time to clean it up. Start by going through the whole house and getting rid of anything that you don't use. There are some methods later in this guidebook that can make the process easier, and you can choose the method that you like the best.

Once the clutter is all gone, you get the benefit of having less to pick up during your cleaning schedule. Simply set up a regular cleaning schedule to keep the house looking nice, and avoid bringing in more clutter at the same time, and you are going to find that it only takes a half hour or so to clean up, rather than the whole day.

5. There is more time for the people and the things that are important to you

The more that you have, the more that you have to waste your time and energy caring for those things. The less that you have, the more time you can spend on the people and things that are really important for you. It may not seem like a big deal to have a few extra items sitting around the house, but think about how much time you are wasting on those items rather than spending your time with the ones you love or doing the things that you love.

When you go through the decluttering process, ask yourself whether you would rather spend your time taking care of that item, or spend time with your loved ones? You may find that this makes it a whole lot easier to throw out some items that you have been holding onto.

6. Some freedom from the scarcity mindset

Many of us are going to do some rationalization when it comes to the items that we convince ourselves to keep. We think that we will use the item later on, or that we may need it at some point. In reality, we don't really need these things at all, we are just focused on a scarcity mindset, or believing that we must hold onto something because we may need it or it can save us money to have that item. Even in a world where there is plenty and no one is starving or constantly looking for food, this scarcity mindset can get us to hold onto things we do not need.

Instead of holding onto those shoes that may look good next spring, but which you haven't worn in three years, or instead of holding onto something "Just in case", it is time to let them go. This can clear up a lot of room in your home and can make life easier.

7. Freedom from holding onto the ideas of the past

Many times we hold onto items because they are about the past. We enjoyed different periods of our lives, times that gave us hope, made us feel good, and were fun. And some of the items that we have can remind us about this time. When an item is tied back to a particular time in our past, it can be even harder to let it go. Instead of hoarding onto that item and letting it take up space in your life, it is much better to let those items go. If they hold a very special place in your heart, take a picture and keep that as proof.

8. Being able to live more in the here and now

There is nothing better than being able to live in the here and now. Too many times we focus on what we need to do in the future, or what has happened in the past. When you focus on decluttering your life, you can let go of some of those things that remind you so much about the past and can help you worry less about how much time you will need to spend on cleaning up your home and your life in the future. You can instead focus your time and attention on the things that you like to do now and the things that make you the happiest now.

9. Can lead to decluttering in other areas of your life, such as your schedule or your mind

Once you figure out how to declutter your home, you can take these lessons and this practice and put it towards other parts of your life. Imagine how nice it would be to have a decluttered schedule, a decluttered mind, and just a decluttered life? If you are successful with decluttering your home, these other aspects of your life will naturally start to fall into place as well.

10. Can help improve your health

Studies have shown how decluttering can actually help to improve your health. There are a number of reasons why this may be true. First, decluttering allows you to have a cleaner home, which is going to make it easier for you to get things done, easier to focus on tasks that you have in front of you, and even easier for you to relax. Many of us don't realize it, but it is really hard to even relax when our homes are messy. With decluttering, you can have an easier time getting your home organized so you can sit back and relax.

Decluttering could also help your health in the fact that you are clearing out some of the attachment that you have to things. Many of us in this consumer world are forming attachments to actual things, like our computers, our phones, pictures, and many other things. We may refuse to declutter our lives because we are slightly attached to them. Being able to let things go can free us up from being so attached to things.

Finally, decluttering can also help reduce your stress levels. Having a home that has a lot of clutter around it can be stressful. Running around trying to find the keys or other things that are needed in the morning can be stressful. All of this can add up to a lot of stress in our lives. Being able to clean out some of the clutter can do wonders for clearing out some of the stress.

Chapter 5:
How to Organize Your Time
to Make Decluttering Easier

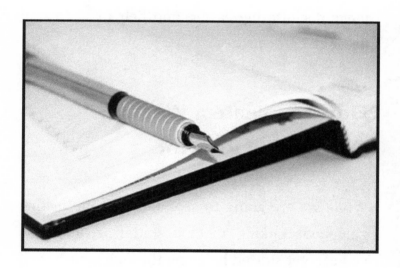

W hen you are ready to get started with the process of decluttering, it is important that you learn how to properly organize your own time. If you are not organized with a good routine and you don't learn the right management techniques, it is easy to feel overwhelmed, get distracted, or have other issues that come up that make it hard for you to actually get the work done. Let's take a look at some of the steps that you can take to make decluttering easier, and helps you to stay on track in the process.

How to Create a Weekly Organizing Routine

While we are going to spend some time in this guidebook talking about decluttering, and how you can get started by going through your home, and keeping or getting rid of things that you need or don't need, you can't just do this once and assume it is going to stay that way permanently. Decluttering and organizing is an ongoing process, and teaching yourself how to stay on this schedule can make a big difference in the results that you get.

Your home, as well as your life, needs a lot of upkeep to help it stay organized. This is especially true when it comes to the process of decluttering. If you don't take the time to declutter on a regular basis, everything is going to pile up and it can become overwhelming. But thinking about organizing your living space can seem daunting.

The best solution that you can stick with is to dedicate a little bit of time every day and then work in 15-minute increments to make this work. You may be surprised at how much you will be able to get done when it comes to decluttering, and organizing any room in your home with just those 15 minutes. Let's take a look at some of the steps that you can take to make this work for you.

First, you should develop your own organizing routine for the week. This routine can be personalized for your needs, but it is meant to help you get through your home, and keep each space decluttered with only spending a few minutes each day. We are going to look at one example, and this one is going to focus a lot on some of the high-traffic areas such as the kitchen, entryway, closet, bedrooms, and bathrooms. You can make the plan as detailed as you would like, but this one is going to include some time for meal planning, meal prep, and laundry as well to make it easier.

Your weekly organization routine is going to include a list of tasks that need to be done each week. You can then pair it with the day that makes the most sense to do this task. Since everyone has a different schedule to follow, your organization routine can be personalized to work with you. But this routine is basically going to be a schedule to keep you on track, with a little bit of flexibility added in so that you can get everything done.

There are a few tools that you can implement into your routine to help you out. You simply need a timer to help you keep track of how much time has passed, a bag or a recycling bin, and a wastebasket and you should be set.

First, there are a few things that you must make sure that you do every day, regardless of what other tasks you have on your list for the week. These things include:

- **First five minutes**: During this time, you can clean off the clutter on the coffee table, bathroom vanity, and kitchen counter. This is a simple sweep that can take all the clutter off and then you put everything back in its place. You can also choose to toss the clutter if it is something that you don't want to keep around.

- **The second five minutes**: Check out your launch pad. This should be the area where you keep important things, such as your incoming and outgoing mail, your cell phone, and keys. You may want to consider having one of these to help you keep some important items in one place so you don't have to search for them all the time.

- **Last five minutes**: This is where you need to clear off the clutter from clothes from rooms where the clothing doesn't belong. This would include clearing the clothes from places like the kitchen, the living room, and the bathroom. You can either put this back into the bedroom or the laundry room until you get to cleaning it.

For the next fifteen minutes or so, it is time to really declutter the room that you have chosen for the day, or do the other task that needs to be done. Some people decide to spend that time quickly going through the rooms of the house, or they will divide up the tasks that need to be done into each day. One day you may clean out the sink or the stove, one you clean the toilets in the bathroom, and another where you fold the laundry. You can set up the schedule that works the best for you.

A routine can be the best thing to help you stay on track when it comes to keeping your decluttering in check. This helps you to make this a habit that you are used to, and can ensure that you get everything cleaned. And it only needs to take fifteen minutes or so a day to see success. Think of all the free time you will have on the weekends if you can keep up with the routine that you set!

Management Tips When Decluttering Your Home

The amount of clutter that you can accumulate in your home can be amazing. Many of us just move it around our homes, making promises that we will get rid of it at some point, but then just moving it around again. It is amazing how much clutter can get into the home and how much of our time is spent dealing with that clutter.

The hardest part about getting started with decluttering is figuring out how to get started. We may look at the process of decluttering our homes and our lives, and then worry that it is such a big task and we will never be able to get it all done. Being able to manage our time and coming up with a plan to tackle it all in a timely manner will help solve this issue. Some of the management tips that you can use when it comes to decluttering your home include:

- **Make a list**: Much like how you would sit down and come up with a grocery list before you go shopping, you should sit down and make a list for each room of what you absolutely need to keep there. This list is going to help you keep on track when you get to work. You can get a good feeling any time that you check something off the list. Now, you may not be able to think of all the items in each room that has to stay, but it helps you have a good idea of what needs to stay and what should go.

- **Go through one room at a time**: Even if you start out with a ton of motivation at the beginning, there is no way you can go through this whole process in one day. This is overwhelming and there is just too much to get done. Instead, just go into one room and make it your goal to get it done. You may be able to get a few rooms done in a day if you get going, but you should not make it your goal to get the entire home done. When you select just one or two at a time, this can help you focus on that space and it just makes your decluttering process easier.

- **Set your time limit**: Have you ever gotten into decluttering and then find that you get distracted looking through an old yearbook or something else that you haven't looked at for a long time? This can be a fun process, but it is not a good idea if you are trying to clean up your home. Before you even take a look at a particular room, set a time limit to get the work done. Twenty to thirty minutes is often plenty to help you get the room done and stay on task.

- **Seasonize**: What this means is that you can organize your items based on the season that you are most likely to use them. You can use some space bags to hide away your sweater in the summer, and some boxes to put away the Christmas decorations. This helps you to keep some of those items that you use during certain times of the year while still decluttering your home at the same time.

- **Get rid of items**: There are several different methods that you can use to get rid of items. You can donate them, you can give them away to friends, or you can try to sell these at a garage sale or online. You can pick any of these options, but make sure that you go through and get rid of those items, rather than letting them sit in a corner for months on end. It doesn't do you a lot of good if your unused and unwanted items just sit there while still being in your home. Get rid of them within a few days after you do the decluttering to help get them out of the home.

- **Make use of the space that you have**: If you look around your home, you are likely to have space that you could use already. Clean out a junk drawer, use a closet after it is cleaned out, or some other space to help you to get the most storage possible in the space that you have.

Chapter 6:
How to Set Your Priorities When Housekeeping and How to Create a Plan

Now that you have gotten the basics of decluttering, you are ready to jump in and see what else you can accomplish if you set your mind to it. Decluttering is a process that can take some time, but the rewards are definitely worth it. Here, we are going to take some time to create a simple decluttering plan so you can get to work, and ensure that your home will be easier to keep clean and that the clutter is finally gone.

Before

There are a few different things that you will need to do before you decide to get started with the decluttering process. Some of the steps that can help you begin include:

- **Write down the date in your calendar**: Yes, you must write it down. It is not enough for you to just say it in your head, you need to write it down to make things official. Set about 30 to 60 minutes for each room in your home. If you plan to do a few rooms, then go ahead and write them both down during the same day. You need to treat these just like any other appointment that you need to handle, so pick a day when you can be free and can devote your whole attention to getting it done.

- **Find someone to help you get it done**: You can either hire someone to be your assistant through this process or find others in your family to help. Having that second pair of hands can keep you company and can make it easier to get through the process. This other person can also help you to stick with your goals and will hold you accountable. It even makes it easier for you to part with some of the items that you may have kept.

- **Have some cleaning products nearby**: You will need to clean as you go to get the most benefits out of this. So grab some cleaning solution, some rags, a dustpan, and a broom to help you get going.

- **Have your lunch (and even supper) prepared ahead of time**: Once you get going with the decluttering, you are going to get focused and trying to get things done. When you finish, or maybe even sometime in the process of cleaning, you will start to feel hungry and want to eat. Having lunch prepared, whether you throw something into the slow cooker, go to a local café, or eat some leftovers, can help you so much once your brain is tired from all the work.

- **Gather up the old boxes and bags that you have**: The bags can be great for gathering up the things that you want to give away as donations. For your time in the kitchen, you may need some newspapers and cardboard boxes to deal with some of the more fragile items.

During

Now that we know a bit about what is needed during the before period, it is time to be prepared for when you actually start to go through the process of decluttering. First, you should begin your decluttering process going category by category. If you do set aside the whole day, then have the goal for that day be tackling the whole wardrobe. If you only have time to do an hour or so of decluttering, then you can pick out some kind of sub-category to help you complete the work in the allotted time.

For example, let's say you only have 30 minutes to devote to this process in one day. You could start by tackling all the jackets in the closet on that day. Grab all the jackets from wherever they may be hiding in the home and put them away nicely. If there is still time, then you could move on the second category, such as cleaning up your shoes. Aim to get as many of these subcategories done in your allotted time.

Now you can work on staging your belongings. Simply by taking all the items and removing them from where you hide them in your home, you are faced with the total volume of all that you own. This can be a kind of shock factor because you may have never realized how many shoes or other items you have at your disposal. This sometimes makes it easier for you to get rid of some of the items. And when you compare some of your older items to some of the newer ones, it is easier to help you throw some of the older ones out. Stage your items first, and then you can go through and make decisions about what you want to keep and what you want to throw out.

After

After you have sorted through all of the items in a particular room, or after you have finished with the decluttering session, there are still a few steps left for you to accomplish. Doing these before you call it quits, can help you to get all those unwanted and unneeded items out of your home, and can provide you with the freedom that you need. Some of the steps that you can take to finish up your decluttering session include:

- **Wrap up the loose ends**: Aim to leave a bit of time at the end of your cleaning session to drop off donations if you can. This may need a bit of extra energy, but doing it right away will ensure those items get dropped off, and that they don't just sit around your home for a long time to come.

- **Recoup some cash if you can**: Depending on the items that you plan to get rid of, you may be able to sell some of them and make some extra money. You may decide to have a garage sale or sell some of the items online and make a few extra bucks. Use this to help pay down some of your debt or to do something fun, but never use that money to go out and purchase more material possessions, or you may be going against all the hard work that you have just done.

The process of decluttering is not meant to be really difficult. Instead, it is meant as a way to make your life easier and less stressful. Setting up a plan and moving from one room to another can really make a difference in how much you can get done, and how overwhelming the whole process can be.

Chapter 7:
The Steps You Need to
Declutter the Kitchen

The first room we are going to take a look at is the kitchen. This is a room that gets a lot of traffic from the family. Not only do we spend time cooking and eating meals in there, but many times it is the place to entertain guests, to work on homework with the kitchen table, and even pay bills and more.

Since the kitchen is such a high traffic area, it can be hard to keep it clutter free and looking nice. This chapter is going to spend some time discussing the simple steps, that you can take in order to help get that kitchen cleaned and spotless and to keep it that way.

Simple Steps to Help You Declutter the Kitchen Quickly

Take a quick look at your kitchen. This is the area where you and your family will dump a lot of stuff, including food, backpacks, mail, and so much more. It is likely that the countertops are crammed with fruit that you need to have eaten, a lot of electronics that are being charged, and even extra appliances, most of which are never used.

This kitchen area can easily get crammed with a lot of stuff, which makes the idea of decluttering feel like a big task. But there are some steps that you can take to help make this process easier. The steps you need for cleaning up the kitchen include:

Set a timer

For most people, it is hard to declutter the whole kitchen in one day. This can be overwhelming and can wear you out quickly. If you are able to do this, then go ahead, but for most people, breaking it up over a few days and doing 30 minutes at a time is a much better option and can keep fatigue at bay. Before you decide to start, go and gather several boxes. You should have a box for relocating, one for items you want to sell, and one for items to donate. You may also need to bring some recycling bags and garbage bags to help with disposal.

When you are ready to start, turn on the time and have it run for the next 30 minutes. Spend your time focusing just on the kitchen and all that you can get done as the time counts down. You can decide at the end whether you would like to go for longer or not.

Focus on just one area at a time

It may seem easy to open up random cabinets in the home and start working, but this can create a lot of chaos and clutter. The best strategy is to open just one cabinet or one drawer. Then go through each item there and figure out whether you would like to keep it or get rid of it. Keep going through this process until that whole drawer or cabinet is taken care of. Make sure that you don't graze through the kitchen and declutter at random though. Take the time to do one area at a time to efficiently clean the kitchen.

Question all of the items you pick up

As you work through the kitchen and are sorting through items, there are a few questions that you should ask yourself including:

- Do I use this?

- How many do I have of this item?

- Would I purchase this item to use today if I saw it at the store?

Be honest with yourself when asking these questions, and don't let the price of something convince you to keep an item that you never use. If you don't actually use that tool or that appliance, then it is just taking up some valuable room, and it is time to get it gone. If you are worried about how much the item originally cost, consider selling it online or at a garage sale to recover some of that lost money.

Remove anything out of the room that doesn't belong there

As you go through the kitchen, you may notice that there are quite a few things that are there that don't really belong. You may see some toys, some clothes, some shoes, some backpacks, old mail, and more. This is a room that seems to catch a lot of the random stuff of the home that should be put elsewhere. This is the step where you take all those items and place them in their proper location in the house.

Kitchen countertops are known for being a big dumping ground for everyone in your home. Grab these items and start putting them away where they belong. If you are in a hurry to get the decluttering done, bring in a box and throw all the stuff that needs to be relocated into this box to deal with later. This still helps you to get that stuff off the counter and out of your way for now.

Set yourself up to reach success.

Even the most simplified kitchen isn't going to be able to stay that way if you don't maintain it on a regular basis. This is why you need to implement a system that can help catch all the clutter that comes in, and there will be clutter over time.

To start with this, look and see what you and other members of your family do in the kitchen. Sure, you spend time cooking and eating in that room, but what other things happen in that room? Do you use it to pay your bills and look up some recipes? Do your kids do some of their homework there as you make supper? The system that you create needs to be able to accommodate all of the tasks that are completed in that room.

For example, if you like to pay bills in the kitchen, then you can dedicate a basket or a bin to store the mail until you can get to it later. If your kids like to spend time doing homework in the room, then dedicate some space to make this easier for them. Keep notebooks, pens, and pencils in a cabinet or a drawer that is out of the way and can hold onto all these items.

Some Easy Tips to Help You Organize the Kitchen

Organizing the kitchen may take a little time, but there are some steps that you can take to ensure that it won't take a week to accomplish. With a few little tricks, you will be able to turn your kitchen into a clean area, one where you can easily find everything that you need in just a few seconds. Some of the tips that you can follow when it comes to decluttering your kitchen include:

- **Create some mini-stations**: This is a good method to go with because it ensures that all similar items stay in one common area. An example of this is if you like to drink coffee. You would then make a refreshment station on a side with everything that is needed to make the coffee. This makes it easier for everyone to be in one place and ensures you won't make a mess of the kitchen in the process.

- **Invest in some baskets**: Baskets can be so nice when it comes to your kitchen. These are great for decluttering the kitchen in a manner that is smart and attractive. You can store any item in them that you want before adding to a cabinet, or you can use hanging baskets to give you more space. They are also really easy to access any time that you want to get an item out of them.

- **Get rid of appliances that you don't use**: This doesn't mean you have to get rid of all your appliances and if you are still using one, then don't get rid of it. But if you have an item that you never use, then they just take up space. If you haven't used one of the items in the last three months in your kitchen, then it is time to donate it or throw it away.

- **Hang up some things**: If you have space and seem to be out of cupboard space way before you think you should, consider hanging up your pans and your pots. This can save some of the space on your shelves and makes the items easier to access, clean, and reuse. You can hang them up on a wall, on the pantry door, or the back of cabinets. There are many no damage hooks or cup holder screws that can help make this easier.

- **Put that lazy space in the kitchen to work**: It is pretty common to waste a lot of space in the kitchen without even realizing it. For example, the space between the cabinet and the ceiling can be put to work for you just like anywhere else. You could construct your cabinet all the way to the ceiling to fix this problem or invest in some storage baskets that can go up there to save your budget and some time.

- **Organize all the shelves**: To do this, you will need to take some time to rearrange things. You can add in some shelves for dinner food, for cereal, and even for some paper products. While working on your shelves, make sure that every item has its own zone so that no matter who comes into your kitchen, they will be able to find the thing they are looking for.

- **Give lids a home**: No one likes to deal with the lids. While we do need them for storage purposes, they often take up a lot of room and just don't seem to fit anywhere nicely. The best way to take care of those lids is to store the lids for your pans and pots separately, to make it easier to access them when you need them most. You can use any space that you want, such as your pantry, a cabinet, or give them their own drawer, just don't store them directly with the pot or pan they go on.

- **Put the items where you are most likely to use them**: You can also divide up your kitchen into specific zones. You should have things like cutting boards, mixing bowls, and other food preparation tools near the largest workspace available in the kitchen. But those items that help with cooking, such as bakeware, pans, potholders, and more, should be near the stove. Then your serving supplies, like napkins, flatware, and dishes, can be near the dining room. Things like foil, Tupperware, and other storage containers do well near the refrigerator and towels, trash bags, and cleaning supplies can work well near the dishwasher. This helps you to put everything in its place and can make it all easily accessible when you need it most.

- **Use the back of pantry and cabinet doors**: Another tip that you can follow when it comes to decluttering your home is to use some clear hanging shoe organizers in your pantry to store a few things. Add it to the back of your pantry door and then hold a ton of items in it such as straws, toothpicks, recipe cards, and more. You can also trim down the organizer if it happens to be too big or wide for what you want to use it for.

Maintaining the Kitchen Clean

After you have put in all of the work above, it is important that you don't let the place become a mess again. It is so easy to do the work and then never touch it again. But if you don't do upkeep in the kitchen, you are going to end up with a room that is messy and cluttered all over again.

Each day, spend about ten minutes in the kitchen. Wipe down the counters after you cook, and wash all of your dishes after every meal. Do a quick sweep through the kitchen at the end of the day, and mop if you feel the floor needs it. Once a month, go through and clean out the fridge and the cupboards, getting rid of any food that may have passed its expiration date, or anything that may be old or you won't use any longer.

Cleaning your kitchen can take up some time. We often throw a lot of knick-knacks in this area and it is hard to sort through everything. Add in that there is so much to sort through between the pantry, the fridge, and all the cupboards, and it can be a big area to work on. But having a plan and dedicating some time to get it done can make all the difference in how much decluttering you get done.

Chapter 8:
Decluttering the Common Living Space

After you have time to work on the kitchen, it is time to move on to the second room in the home — the living room. This is a place where your family gathers to spend time together. It is a place where you can share a lot of memories. It is also a place that a lot of people are going to see first when they come into your home. Making sure that it is neat and tidy can make a big difference in how people perceive your home, and how messy the rest of the home is.

Since you and your family spend so much time in the living room, it is not surprising that so much clutter can accumulate there. Being able to handle the clutter and getting rid of everything that is just in the way can make a big difference. Let's look at some of the steps that you can take to help declutter your living room and make it feel more comfortable and inviting.

How to Declutter the Living Room

When you are ready to clean out your living room, there are a few things that you can do to make the process easier. First, you will want to begin with dusting. You can either get some good dusting spray and a cloth to wipe down everything, or invest in a vacuum that can help do this as well. Go through and dust off everything in that area to make it look a bit nicer. Clean off the tables and end tables as you go and either throw things away or put them where they belong, such as a newspaper stand for all your magazines and books.

Next, take a look at the shoes that are in the way. It is best if you and your family members get into the habit of taking your shoes off before you enter the home. But in some cases, this doesn't happen. Clear the shoes out of the room and put these items in their own personal spot in the home. Take a look at how many shoes are in your living room as well. If one pair keeps being brought out but is never really worn, it may be time to throw it away.

Paper paraphernalia can really take over the living room as well. Newspapers, magazines, school work, mail, and more can be everywhere. Go through and pick all of this up off the floor and get rid of anything that you don't need right then and there. You can then pick up any books that are on the floor, as well as any magazines and other similar items that are in the way.

And now, it is time to deal with the clutter in your living room. Take a moment to think of some of the places in your living room that tends to accumulate a lot of clutter. The coffee table can be to blame, end tables, shelves, and more.

Clear off the clutter at this time to help you get rid of anything that is in the way there. Decide whether you want to keep the item or not, and then place it where you want it to stay.

Take another look around the room and determine what else needs to be handled. If there are still items that are in the way, then you need to decide if you want to keep them or not. If you decide to keep them, then find a place for those items right away. If you don't want to keep those items, then now is the time to get rid of them.

After you have had time to clean up all the mess on the floor and in the rest of the home, it is time to vacuum. Take your time with this and get all the dust and junk off the floor. This process should be done at least once or twice a week to help maintain the decluttering that you have done, and to help keep the carpet in good working order. If you have time, and a few times a year as well, consider doing a carpet clean as well to really finish up the room.

The Four Looks Decluttering Method

Now it is time to get into the basics of decluttering your living room. To start, take a look around the room and see what things are obviously trash (such as wrappers, tissues, and so on) that you need to throw away from the beginning. A good approach is to start in one corner and then slowly move through the room. After you pick up all the trash on the floor, you can look through the room again and see which items that look like clutter, and which you want to get rid of right now. This isn't something to overthink. Just go for the things that you know for sure are clutter right off the bat and then get rid of those particular items.

The first two passes should be pretty quick but can clean up a lot of the room at the same time. Now you can look for the third time, and see what items are in the room that doesn't belong there, and needs to put somewhere else in the home. This may be shoes, hair brushes, and so on. Take your time to pick these things up. You can either go and put them away right this second, or you can place them in a box to deal with when you are all done.

At this point, do a fourth look through and see what is still left in that room. Does everything fit there and look like it belongs, or is there still a cramped feeling in the room? If you still feel like there is too much stuff in that space, then it is time to make the hard decisions and you must really go through and decide what can stay and what goes. Be serious with yourself in determining what you would like to keep so that room becomes less cluttered.

After this time, the living room should be picked up and more organized. You should have everything put where it belongs, in other parts of the home or in that room, and you should have gotten rid of all the items that needed to be thrown away. When you look around the living room, you should notice that there is more room to breathe and it doesn't feel as cluttered any longer.

Tips to Help You Get Even More Out of Your Living Room

- **Dare to be spare**: With too much furniture, even a living room that is big can look very cramped and crowded. Ease out some of that congestion by keeping things basic. You really only need a few items like a coffee table, an end table, a chair, a bookshelf, and a sofa. If you have a television, get a simple stand for it or consider doing a wall hookup to save even more room.

- **Get rid of all the pileup**: Many people subscribe to some magazine or another, and then they hold onto the past issues of that magazine. This can create a big pileup in your home that is hard to handle. You need to become ruthless with this pileup because all it is doing is taking up your space. Save only the last two issues, or even just one issue of a magazine. If you have an article you want to save, tear it out of the magazine and store in a binder for later.

- **Keep the room clean**: You need to keep the living room maintained, or it won't be long before you are back in the same situation you had when you started. A good rule to remember is that you should always be able to see a minimum of 75 percent of your coffee table.

- **Control the remotes**: If you have a few remotes in your home, group them all together in a decorative bowl or a lidded box. This keeps them from making a mess all over your living room and can make it easier for you to find them later.

- **Cut out some of the pillows**: You do not need to have fifty pillows in your living room. This takes up a lot of space and can make it difficult to keep the area clean. A trio in complementary patterns and colors, with one being solid, can be just fine for most sofas. You may want to consider cutting all pillows out to save clutter and room.

- **Double up**: Make sure that you are maximizing storage and get some extra seating at the same time. Use an ottoman to help you hide stuff inside. This allows you to store pillows, blankets, and more, while still having an extra spot to sit in your living room.

- **Floor show**: Having too many area rugs has a way of chopping up the room visually. Instead, you can consider layering a statement rug over carpeting or over your bare floors.

- **Rule of three**: When you are working on what to put away on a shelf, restrict any items that are not books to only three per each shelf. The shapes and sizes can vary, but try to relate them by theme or color to make the area look nicer.

- **Lighten up your library**: Yes, you may love to read, but this doesn't mean you need to hang on to each book you have ever read. Try to reduce your library as much as you can, and consider moving some onto your e-reader to get the best results.

Your living room is an area that lots of people in the family gather and spend time together in, and it is often a room that a lot of people are going to notice when they come to see your home. Make sure that you take the time to declutter your living room, and get it to look nice with the help of the tips that we listed above!

Chapter 9:
The Dreaded Bathrooms
and How to Make Them
More Manageable

The bathroom is one area of the home that most people do not want to spend their time cleaning. This room often has a lot of different items that are all over the place, and cleaning it up can take a lot of time and elbow grease. But it is possible to clean up the bathroom as well and make it more manageable than before. This chapter is going to take a look at some of the things that you can do to help clean up and declutter your bathroom to save a lot of time when getting ready in the morning.

The ABC's of bathroom storage

When it comes to your bathroom, there are a lot of little things that you need to worry about storing. And many of them are used on a semi-regular basis. You may not need them all the time, but you need them often enough that you don't want to get rid of them at all. This is where the ABC of storage can come into play and help you see some great results. It allows you to sort things out based on how much you use them, and it also keeps the bathroom as organized as possible. The way that you follow this method includes:

"**A**" storage areas are the ones that are active, easy to access, and hold onto items that are meant to be used all the time, or on a daily basis. When we are in the bathroom, this could include things like the shampoo bottle, the razor, a blow dryer, and the toothbrush. The areas that fit here should be really user-friendly and you want to be able to reach them without any hidden hazards. The mesh bucket in the shower, the top drawer of your sink, or the countertop can all be great places to store these items.

"**B**" storage areas are going to hold onto items that you may not use each day, but you use weekly or monthly. This area could include some things like nail care equipment, scrunchies, beard trimming kit, and so on. You want these to still be pretty easy to access, but they don't need to be on the top shelf or anything. Places that would count here include above the toilet storage, a cupboard, under the sink, or even in the middle drawer.

Then there are the "**C**" storage areas. These are going to require more stretching, standing, and bending to get the item. These are things like your fancy makeup, the hot foot massage machine, and other things that you use occasionally, but not necessarily on a regular basis. If you use the item more than two times a year, but fewer than once a month, then it fits in this category. These are going to be put in the places that you don't spend much time in, but somewhere that you can still access when you need them

Now, when you are ready to go through the items that you have in the bathroom, bring along a box as well. Not only will you go through and sort out all your items into the three categories that we talked about above, as well as throwing some of them away. Be careful about the items that you decide to keep and which ones you actually need to throw away.

Trash bags can be useful as well. Take everything that is in your bathroom out of the drawers and cupboards and everywhere else. Then slowly go through and throw things into the different containers. Choose what you want to keep, separating out into A, B, and C, what you want to get rid of, and what you want to store in another location, such as in a hall closet.

Everything should have a place when you are done and everything should be back in place. This is not a room to hold things off as undecided because there often isn't a lot of room around to store these things. Make a decision about the things that you use, and the things that you don't, and then put them all away in the right spot.

With all the items that go into the bathroom, it is sometimes tempting to say that you use an item and need to keep it. But remember that the amount of space that you have in your bathroom is pretty limited, even with adding in some storage, and you don't need to keep everything. In most cases, you could probably be just fine with the A category items and maybe a few B, and then throwing everything else away. At a minimum, make sure you go through your bathroom and get rid of anything that you haven't used in at least the last year. You will be surprised at how much the clutter will go away when you do this.

When you are all done sorting through the items in your bathroom and making it look better, take some time to clean things off. Get those cleaning supplies ready and clean off the counter, the floor, the shower, and the toilet, and everywhere else that needs some attention in your bathroom. Then close the door feeling good that you did a great job making the area look nice.

Some Tips to Make Decluttering Your Bathroom Easier

The bathroom is a room that most people don't want to deal with. It can be messy, and if you go a long time without picking up, it may be a bit disgusting. If you take the time to declutter the room, you will find that it doesn't take so much time to keep the bathroom clean afterward. Some of the things that you can consider doing in order to help declutter the bathroom, and keep it organized for the long term include:

- **Work on the medicine cabinet**: Get rid of any containers that are empty, or any that contain medicines that are old and outdated. Check to see which medications are ones you don't even use anymore and throw those out as well.

- **Only keep the things you use daily in the bathroom**: Things like the hairbrush and toothbrush can stay in the bathroom. But while a first-aid supply kit is important, it is just taking up space in the bathroom since you don't use it on a regular basis. Find a new home for this kind of stuff.

- **Store the straighteners and hair dryers in a file organizer**: If you use a lot of things to help get your hair ready in the morning, you know how much room their cords can take up. Take a magazine rack or file organizer and attach it to the side of the bathroom sink, or even on the inside of your cabinet door.

- **Consider a magnetic strip**: This magnetic strip can help you hold onto your nail filer, nail clippers, bobby pins, and tweezers. Instead of searching around all the time to find these, attach a magnetic strip inside your medicine cabinet and add all these items there.

- **Use Mason jars to store brushes and toothbrushes**: This can be a great way to make sure that you get everything stored without having them roll around and cause a mess. Plus, you can easily choose from different options and even colors in order to get the look that you want.

- **Add a shelf above the door**: Many bathrooms are short on storage space. But this doesn't mean you can't add in a little bit of your own. Adding in a shelf above the bathroom door, an area you aren't using anyway could be the perfect way to get the results that you want. It doesn't have to be a very big one, just big enough to store a few extra items.

- **Consider using a tray organizer**: A tray organizer, like what you see with your forks, spoons, and other utensils, can also work when it comes to organizing your bathroom. You can add in your toothbrushes, makeup brushes, and more to this organizer, making it easier for you to see where everything is, without worrying about them rolling all over the place.

- **Use a tension rod to hold onto the cleaning products**: Go under your sink and add in a little tension rod. This can be fitted to the size that you need and is a great way to put your cleaning products under the sink without them being in the way or worrying about them falling over. Then, when it is time to clean the mirror, the counters, the toilet, or the floor, you can just reach under the sink and get exactly what you need.

- **Attach a nice spice rack to one of the bathroom walls**: Think about some of those spice racks that you already have in your kitchen. These are a nice way to get those spices off the bottom of your cabinets and can free up so much space. The same can be said when you use them in your bathroom. Attach one to a wall that makes the most sense in your bathroom and store a few things on it.

These are just a few of the different options that you can use in order to free up some space in your bathroom and can help you get that area as organized as possible. The bathroom can be a really hard area to clean up because it is often smaller, and still has to hold onto a lot of different items. When you figure out how to properly store some of those items and you find ways to add in some more storage, you are going to see some great results in how organized your bathroom is.

Remember that when you are done with cleaning up the bathroom, take some time to set up a maintenance schedule to keep the bathroom as clean as possible. Make sure that you wipe all the counters down, clean the toilet, and do a quick clean of the floor as well. A little maintenance on a daily basis can make it easier for you to get some great results when it comes to your bathroom and can make this room a little less of a chore.

Chapter 10:
Cleaning Up the Bedrooms

D
o your bedrooms often feel cluttered and like there is a ton of stuff hanging around all the time, things that you have to walk around and push out of the way just to get to bed? If so, one of the best things that you can do is declutter the room and get rid of things that are just in your way. When you

remove all the clutter, the room is going to feel spacious and open, and you will have a much better chance of feeling relaxed.

A bedroom is going to be a catchall many times. When you are cleaning the other rooms of the home, you may inadvertently put a lot of random things in your room and then forget they are there. Instead of dealing with the problem, you will keep pushing things around until the room is a mess. You may need to take some time to deal with the mess in your bedroom, so set aside a few days to get it done. Let's take a look at some of the things that you can do to help declutter the bedrooms in your home.

Getting Rid of the Extra Things that are in your Room

The first step that you should take is to grab a trash bag and then go through your whole room. You are going to need at least a few to keep track of all the different trash and garbage that is there. Start with the trash that is lying around on the floor and taking up space, and then move on to items that may be broken, or ruined linens and clothes. If you are not sure whether you want to throw an item away, then create a 'maybe pile' to go through later on.

Next, you need to focus on anything that doesn't belong. You can then spend the next ten minutes or so going through the bedroom and getting rid of anything that shouldn't be in your room. Look for things like loose change, paperwork, and dishes. Clear out the areas that are even out of sight, like in between the furniture and under the bed.

The best thing that you can do here is to remove these completely out of the bedroom. You can set up a pile that is out of the room for any trash or miscellaneous belongings. Then you can take those items and place them in the right spot when you are ready so you don't end up adding clutter in a different room.

- Now you can take some time to go through your drawers. Take out a drawer and remove all of the items that are inside. Go through each drawer one at a time. Then make up three piles with the things that are in each drawer. Have a pile for garbage, one for donate, and one for things you want to keep. Once you get one drawer done, put all of the "keep" items back inside. Continue this process for every drawer you do.

- When this process is done, you can move the garbage items to the trash. Place the pile to donate in a bag and have it ready to take out soon. You can also offer any items that you want to get rid of to others you know.

- If you are in doubt about an item, then throw it away and free up some room. It is fine to hold onto a few sentimental items if you want, but be careful about holding onto too many items.

- Set up a drawer or space in the room for any of the sentimental objects that you want to keep. This could include items like clothes, ticket stubs, drawings, and letters.

- Decide if the sentimental thing is worth your time to keep it or not. It may have some good memories, but if you have something else that will remind you of that event, or that memory isn't that important for you, then it is time to get rid of the item.

Now you can work on clearing off all the surfaces. Go through the end tables, dresser, and more, and get rid of all the belongings that are just lying around. Throw away anything that you don't want to keep anymore and the only things that you really want to keep in your room should be things like a computer, a lamp, or other types of décor. When everything is put back in place and you get rid of the things you no longer need, it is time to clean off the area. Dust and wipe off anything that needs it.

You can now work on sorting through the clothes that you have. You can work on your wardrobe and decide which items you would like to keep. Take everything out of the dresser and the closet and then sort it all out. You can sort through what you want to donate, what you want to throw out, and what you want to keep. Then you can organize the clothes based on whether they need to go back into the closet or the dresser to make them easier to access.

After everything has been thrown out or ready to donate or put back away, it is time to organize your room. Consider if you want to rearrange the room at all and move the furniture so that it makes the most sense. Even if you don't want to permanently change up the room, it may be a good idea to move things a bit so that you can clean and vacuum under it to make it look nice. We will talk about cleaning the closet later on, but you may want to reorganize this part as well to make it easier to find things.

Another idea is to install shelves. Shelves are a great way to help you add a bit of extra storage so you can keep some of the clutter from the floor. You can go to a hardware store and find some shelving holders that are easy to mount to the bedroom wall, so they don't take up any more space than necessary in your room. Make sure that the shelves are placed high off the ground so you don't have to worry about running into them.

Another option to consider is to use storage furniture. There are plenty of options for furniture that can act as a storage unit. These are helpful if you are limited in closet space and you want to be able to fit linens and other supplies. You can find a lot of options such as a bed frame that has some drawers under the bed, a dresser, and more.

Keeping Up with the Maintenance of the Cleaning

An important thing to remember when you get started on this process is that you need to maintain the clutter-free zone. It won't do you a lot of good to just start throwing things back on the floor right after you are done. You need to spend a bit of time each day, maybe even just five minutes, cleaning up the bedroom to make it look nice.

The first step is to make sure that your laundry gets put away after it is done. A common way for some of the clutter to build up again is after you are done with laundry. Many people will just shove it into their room and forget about it.

Instead of doing this, you can fold the laundry right when it is done and then put it away immediately. Never let piles of clothing build up in your room. If you find that you don't have enough room for these clothes, then it is time to go through them again and get rid of a few things. If you need some storage for items that are more seasonal, then you can get a storage bin and place it in the attic, the garage, or under the bed.

Take the time to clean up the room on a regular basis as well. Rather than cleaning your room just once a year, take the time to do small bits of cleaning or organizing every day of the week. If you have a bit of clutter in the corner of the room or on the desk, then take the time to clean it up. Never let a small mess accumulate into a big one. You can save yourself a lot of hassle in the future by tackling a little bit of clutter as it forms. You should plan to vacuum or sweep the room at least one time a week.

And finally, you need to make sure that you avoid overbuying anything in the future. It doesn't do you a lot of good to clear out the clutter in your room and then going back out and purchasing a ton of stuff all over again. Hoarding materials and purchasing an impulse buy can make this different. It is time to limit how many belongings you are allowed to purchase.

The next time that you consider going out and purchasing something, take a few minutes to think about where you would put that item in your room. You may think about the stuff that you already have and decide that it is not a good thing to purchase. And if you are considering that it is time to upgrade a belonging, then you should decide whether or not you are willing to get rid of the original of that item.

Cleaning your bedroom can sometimes be the most difficult, because you may keep a lot of personal touches around the room, and a lot of sentimental items there. This can take some time to go through everything and figure out what you would like to keep and what to get rid of. It is fine to keep a few of the decorations around your room, a few pictures, and maybe a few sentimental items. But you need to make sure that you actually have room for them, and that they don't become unnecessary clutter in your room.

Chapter 11:
Watch Out for Those Lego! – How to Declutter Your Kids' Rooms

In addition to cleaning out your other bedrooms, you will also want to take time to clean out the rooms that your kids play in. These rooms will need some special attention to help keep them clean, and it may be a good idea to involve your child in doing some of the work. This ensures that they understand the process that is going on, and will be willing to help out and keep the room clean. Some of the things that you can do when it comes to cleaning your kids' bedroom will include:

Get your kids involved with the process from the beginning.

It is not a good idea to just walk into your child's room and start throwing things away. You need to involve them in the process and work with them before you go through and re-organize the room. Kids as young as three want to participate and some can even find it exciting to be involved in this way. You may worry that a child is going to be frustrated or bored when you talk about decluttering a room, but they see it as a way that they can talk about their toys and get attention from their parents.

In addition, when you get your child involved in the organizing process, they are going to be more willing to let you get the work done. They will feel like they have some ownership on the project, and they are more likely to keep things in order when things are done.

Ask your kid to give you a tour before you start

Never just walk into your child's room and start throwing things away or getting rid of them. It is best to take it slowly and let your child feel like they are the ones in control. Consider starting with letting your child show you what is in their room. This gives you a sense of the tone and language the child will use towards certain things and can give you a good idea of what that child finds the most important.

Really listen to what the child tells you and try to mimic back some of the behavior if you can. This makes it easier for them to trust that you are on their side and that you aren't there just to take their stuff away. Remember that even though these toys are just items, your child has personified them a bit and may feel a connection with them. This is not a bad thing. They don't have the same kind of connection that adults give to items. Listening to your child and figuring out what is valuable to them and how they are feeling at the time can help you be more successful with this endeavor.

Discuss how all the stuff in the room must have a home.

Kids are a bit different than adults in that they have a great ability to personify the things around them. So, one method that you can use is asking your child "Where should we give this a home?" when you work on organizing with them. Many times we get caught up in the idea of saying that it is time to put one item or another away, and this can feel very negative to a child. Instead, you could say something like "Can we put that where it lives?" It is a simple change that actually makes a world of difference to a child.

Give permission for the kid to let go of anything they don't want or use.

Sometimes, the volume, or the amount of stuff in the room, can be overwhelming for your child. But many kids don't know that it is just fine to say no to things they no longer want. They may be worried that they are doing something bad by throwing out or getting rid of the items. Give your child permission to let go of items they don't want, no matter what that item may be. Consider helping them to donate the items to a charity so there is more positivity that comes with letting go of items.

Start from the bottom up

Another thing to consider is where to start. And with younger children, starting on the ground is a great idea because it helps them to see the work that you are doing. The bottom-up strategy will take the process of decluttering down to the level of your kid, and helps them stay grounded in the task at hand. Plus, if your child can see where the homes for their items are, this can make it easier for them to develop the habit of placing them there.

Reinforce the routine that you are setting up with cubbies

You will find that a great tool that you can use is cubbies. These can help kids organize so well, and can kind of give them an experience like they are at school. You can place the cubbies anywhere that they make the most sense in your home, but the entryway of the room can be nice. This becomes a natural drop zone for your child. The cubby allows your child to drop off their stuff, without thinking about it and without making a huge mess everywhere.

Count to ten

Remember that when your children are helping you out, games are really fun and can help make things easier. When things get messy in the bedroom, make the process of cleaning up feeling like it is a game or play. One game can be to have your child count backward and then get them to pick up ten items to place back in their homes at the end of the day. This can make the chore sound more like a game rather than work, and it can reinforce this good habit in your child at a young age.

Make sure that you lead by example

This is something that you should do no matter which room of the home you are cleaning. If you want your kids to keep their rooms clean and uncluttered, then you need to do the same thing. Kids are going to mirror what their parents do. If you take the time to go through and declutter the home, this is going to reflect in the work that the kids do as well. Every moment is a lesson with your kids so make sure you develop good decluttering habits as well so that your children learn what is expected.

Cleaning out the room that your kid sleeps in can be an extra challenge. This is their personal space, a place where they not only sleep and dream, but where they hold onto some of their own personal belongings. You need to go through and take some extra steps to make sure that this room is as clean and clutter free as possible.

Chapter 12:
Working on the Office for a More Effective You

T he next room that you can take a look at is the home office. This is a special room in the home because each person is going to use it a bit differently. Some will use it to conduct their actual business, and others may use it as a place to relax, a place to keep track of bills, or even a place to store books and other materials. With so many different uses of the home office, it can take some time to actually go through and declutter this room. This chapter is going to spend some time talking about the home office, and providing you with the steps you need to make this room as orderly as possible.

Identify How You Plan to Use the Office and What is the Most Important

Working from home or having a home office can be a great way to help you stay organized and get things done. But each person is going to use that office in a slightly different manner. But it is hard to do any decluttering in a space when you have no idea how you are going to use that space. If you don't know how you will use the space, then how would you know which items shouldn't and should be found there.

Before you go through the process of decluttering, it is important for you to have a clear picture of what activities already take place, or will take place in that home office. To start, grab a pen and some paper and write down all the ways that you currently use that space. The results of this exercise may provide some good insights to you and can make the decluttering process a bit easier. Some ideas to consider regarding your home office are whether it is a place to:

- Use your printer and computer

- Store journals, magazines, or books

- Store work materials, office supplies, and physical files

- Prepare or collate materials

- Administrative items or process paperwork

- Have webinars, virtual meetings, and telephone calls

- Brainstorm some new ideas

- Review materials

- Think quietly without a bunch of interruptions

- Meet with clients

You can see from this list that there are a ton of things that you can do in your home office, and each of them will allow different items to be found there. Take some time to decide what activities you already do in the office or which ones you plan to do in the future before you go through the process of decluttering that room.

Remove Anything that is a Household or Personal Item

When you look at your desk, one of the first things that you may notice is that there are a ton of household and personal items around. These may be on, or around your desk, or in other places around the room. There are many reasons why these items end up in your office, but since they aren't related to the work that you are doing, they need to be removed.

Start this process by rounding up all of these household and personal items. These may include things like exercise gear, equipment, books, kitchenware, small appliances, toys, accessories, shoes, and clothing. Depending on how the rest of your office looks, you may need to look around and do a bit of cleaning in order to find some of these unnecessary items. Don't just look at the floor and on the desk to find them. You may need to look under equipment racks and the desk, in storage chests and closets, and even in your filing cabinets and desk drawers to find these items.

Once you have had some time to gather these items, you need to take them and return them back where they really belong in the home. For instance, if you are putting clothing away, put it back in the closet or dresser where it belongs. The toys can go back in your child's room, and the kitchen items can head on back to the kitchen.

Declutter the Workstation

While it is fine to use office supplies and keep a few personal items at the workstation, you want to make sure that these items aren't so plentiful that you are drowning in them when you should be getting things done. The workspace is your location to get work done, and it should never become a magnet for all that clutter.

To start, take a good look at your workstation. If you need to, get up out of the chair and walk away a bit. This helps you take in the full picture of your workstation and what needs to happen. Consider what the workstation looks like. What is near, beside, behind and on top of your desk, and your chair? Which of those items and which materials and supplies do you use on a daily basis? Which items can you store in another place in your office and which ones can be thrown out?

The first thing to do is throw away anything that is extra on the desk. You can bring in a trash bag to help make this easier. Make it a goal to get rid of at least ten items on the desk that don't belong there. You probably don't need to keep the newspaper from earlier that week or all those extra magazines. There are probably some notes on the desk from past appointments or projects that you don't really need at all either. Throw away all the clutter.

Once that is done, you can move on to sorting through the things that you need to keep. Getting some color-coded folders and other organizational tools can help with this. This helps you to put away the remaining papers and notes and still ensures that the stuff that goes together, such as notes and papers on a specific project, stay together. You can choose the organizational method that you want to go with, just make sure that it removes the clutter and keeps everything as organized as possible.

Make a Checklist for Decluttering

If you want to make sure that your office is running the best it can and that you won't run into a lot of distractions, then you want to make sure that you keep up with a series of decluttering tasks that you can do on a regular basis. You can include these into your regular work routine to make things easier. Keeping track of the tasks that you want to get done can be as simple as creating a checklist. Aim to take care of these items on a monthly or a weekly, and sometimes even on a daily basis, to ensure that the materials and the mess don't have time to build up on you.

If your office seems to be a magnet for clutter, then take some time each week to do a decluttering session. You can add this into your schedule just like with any other important appointments that you need to take care of. Consider doing it at the end of the week so you have time to get it done, and can have a clean and clear workspace when you come back the following week.

There are a lot of tasks that you can add to your checklist to help you keep your office space looking neat and tidy. The tasks that you choose to do to clean up the home office will vary based on the way that you choose to use that room. Some may choose to use it as an extra room in the home to store important things, and others may find that it works best for them to conduct their business, whether it is a traditional or stay at home job. Some of the items that you may wish to include are:

- Remove any of the personal items that have made it into the office and shouldn't be there.

- Declutter underneath, on the side, and on the top of your desk, or any other area you are working on.

- Pull out old or expired papers and digital files, and get rid of any that you don't need.

- Toss out any assignment materials, programs, and projects that are old.

- Shred the materials and paperwork that need to remain confidential.

- Clean out folders and files from the desktop screen of your computer.

- Declutter your email accounts and folders.

Decluttering out your office is so important for helping you to get more work done, and ensuring that things aren't given time to add up. A clean and clear workspace can make all the difference when it comes to how well you can get the work done. Spend less time trying to find the things that you need, and more time actually getting work done when you implement some decluttering into your week.

Chapter 13:
Cleaning Out the Garage
and the Basement

The next two rooms that we are going to talk about are the basement and the garage. These two areas need to have some special attention because they can often be a big mess of clutter. Many people choose to just throw random items in these rooms, items that they want to get out of the way and hope to deal with later, but then they never do.

Because of all this clutter and a lot of time being abandoned, these areas may take some extra time. But with a little bit of planning and taking things in zones, you will be able to clear them out and give yourself a lot of extra space to do what you enjoy. This chapter is going to take some time to show you the basics of cleaning out your garage and your basement so you can finally reclaim those areas for your own needs.

Decluttering the Garage

First, we are going to take some time to talk about the steps that you can take to declutter your garage. The garage is one area that can attract a lot of mess if you are not careful. Many times, it gets so full of things and so cluttered, that it could be difficult to even get the car through the door. Add in that you often hold a lot of tools, bikes, gardening and yard supplies, and more in there, and it is no wonder that this area will quickly become a mess.

There are a few things that you can do to help clear out the garage. This will give you a lot more space and ensures that you are actually able to get the car into the garage each day. Some of the best tips that you can follow to help declutter your garage include:

- **Take all the items out**: At least get all of the items that you can safely remove out of the garage. This helps you to get a good idea of what was in the garage to start and you can move on from there. Clear out everything, or at least as much as possible.

- **Sort through your finds and work to put similar things together**: This is a really important step when you are trying to make sure that there is some extra space in the garage. For example, put all the hardware together, all the gardening tools, the sporting equipment, and the tools. Do not start putting them back in the garage yet, just leave them in groups so you get a better idea of what you all own.

- **Purse:** After you get everything grouped together, you should have a good idea of what items you own and how many. You may be surprised to see that you have six hammers, and all of them are similar. If this is true in your garage, you should get rid of them. If you have a lot of duplicates of items, or there are lots of damaged items, then get rid of them. This alone may help you to drastically cut down on how many items are in your garage.

- **Organize**: After you have gone through each item that is in your garage, then decide on the things that you want to keep. Now it is time to make a plan of how you would like to store these items so they are easy to get, and will maximize the amount of space that you have. You may want to get a tool cabinet, a pegboard, or even storage bins, and some garages need shelving to help. Try to create a nice storage space in the garage that is off the ground, and can hold some of the items that you have. As you start to put things back away, make sure to label everything so that it is easy to find the items when you need them later on.

- **Rent out some more storage space**: It is preferable if you are able to clean out enough of the clutter in your garage that you can easily fit everything back in there. But in some cases, the garage may be too small or there is some other reason that you just can't fit everything back in there. If this sounds like your garage, then it may be time to rent out some extra storage space. This can help to clear up some extra space around the home and around your garage as well.

Working on your garage can take a bit of time. There are often a lot of items that find their way to the garage, including items for doing the yard work and even boxes of unused items from the home. Make sure that you can spend a few hours in this area so that you can give it the time that it deserves. It is fine for you to split it up into zones as well, to ensure that you are able to get little parts done in the time frame that you have available.

Cleaning out the garage can be an eye-opener. Many times when we follow the steps above, we are going to find that we own a lot of extra items that we never knew we had. Often just combining same items together is enough to empty out a lot of the garage, and if you throw out any item that is damaged or not working well, or that you want to update at a later time, the garage will quickly empty itself out without you missing out on much!

Decluttering the Basement

The basement can be a difficult area to work with. It often catches a lot of the items that we just box up and put away to get out of sight. But on occasion, it is still a good idea to clear it out to make more room, and to get rid of the things that are just sitting in the way. Some of the steps that you can follow to help you get rid of the clutter in your basement include:

1. **Divide up the basement into zones**: It is important to just work on one part of the basement at a time, especially if the area is large. You can work in one room, on a set of shelves, on the seasonal

decorations, on old toys and clothes, or some other part. But just do one thing at a time so you don't become overwhelmed in the process.

2. **Take everything out of the zone**: Let's say that you decided to start with the shelves first. Then the first thing you need to do is take everything off the shelves. If you are working on bins or boxes, then empty the bins out. You should never move on to a second or third zone until you are done with that current zone.

3. **Sort out everything in the basement into two bins**: Since you are in an area that is reserved for storing things, you can remove one of your bins and then focus on either getting rid of or keeping the items that you find there. If you find things that you want to fix, then create a third bin for

items that you can affordably fix. Make sure these have a deadline though, so you don't end up holding onto them for years to come. If you are uncertain about whether you will actually ever fix that item or not, then it is best to just throw it away.

4. **Move the items that you don't plan to keep outside the home**: Before you even think about putting away the items that you would like to keep, take the ones that you choose to get rid of and move them out of the home. Put them right into the trash if you plan to throw them away, or take them to the donation center. This ensures that you get them out of the way and that you don't just shove them right back into the same place again.

5. **Keep things that are similar together**: This is a tip that applies to any room in the home that you are trying to declutter. When you store similar things together, it makes it easier for you to find and access them anytime that you need them down the road. So, put all the Christmas decorations together, all the seasonal clothes together, and so on, to make it easier to find them.

6. **Label the bins and the boxes**: After you have taken the time to sort through the basement, make sure to label everything as you put it back. The better you can label, the easier it will be to find these items later on if you need them. Any type of label will do, just make sure that you are able to see it, that it fully describes what is in that bin or box, and that it won't get ruined down the road.

Cleaning out your basement can take some time. There is often a lot of junk and miscellaneous stuff down there, stuff that you just put down there to get it out of your way. It is fine to spend a few days in this area because it is often a big undertaking, but if you work through each zone one at a time, you are going to see the results. Also, consider the different areas or zones that you would like to set up when you get started with this process. For example, if you have a lot of decorations for the different holidays, consider which zone will work the best for this, so that you can place all of those items next to each other to find them easier later on.

This area can also be difficult because of the number of sentimental things that may be stored down there. Before putting that heirloom back in the box, consider whether you would actually use that in the future and if you actually like the item. If you are just keeping it around because of obligation, then it is time to dump it out. Clearly label everything when you put it back and make sure that it is put away in an orderly fashion, and you will find that it is easier than ever to have a clean basement where everything is easy to find.

Chapter 14:
How to Make That Closet
Look Organized

After you have taken some time to clean out all the other rooms in your home, it is time to take a look at the closet. The closet is often the room where you just throw random things that are in the way. And maybe you threw a few items in here as you were decluttering some of the other rooms. Even if you were good about not throwing items into the closet as you cleaned, it is likely that there is still some clutter in these areas from before, and it can be a big eyesore any time you open the door.

But now it is time to open up those closet doors and see what you can do about that mess. Yes, even your closet can be decluttered if you know the right steps to take, and it doesn't have to be as scary as you may think. Let's take a look at some of the tricks that you can employ when it is time to work on decluttering your closet to make the process a bit easier.

Take just one hour

When you take a look at your closet, you may be overwhelmed by all that needs to get done. There are clothes all over the floor, there are shoes that are everywhere, and you see that purses, blankets, and other things are just hanging around as well. This can make you feel like the work will never be done. One of the best things to do here is to just schedule an hour at a time to help make a dent in that messy closet.

To make this work, bring out a timer and set it for 60 minutes. Or if you can't spare that much time in your busy schedule, split it up into two

30 minute increments through the week. During that time, you just get as much done as possible. Bring in some trash bags to throw broken and old stuff in, as well as some boxes to hold any items that you plan to donate.

This time period is just devoted to working on the closet and getting the following steps done. You should not have any other plans going on at the same time, and if the kids are going to interrupt you often, then it may be best to set up a play date or have someone watch them so you can get your work done. When the timer is done, it is time to stop where you are, put things away, and come back to the work later on.

Take everything out of the closet

This may seem like a task, but it can really help you get started. You want to take every last thing that is in the closet out. If you don't take the time to do this, then chances are that the same unworn clothes are just going to be moved around in the closet, rather than being taken care of.

Once you get all the items out of your closet, it is time to sort through it all. Throw out any shoes that are damaged, purses that have missing straps or that are torn, and clothing that is damaged and old. Don't assume that you will fix it up to use later, because you probably won't put in the time to actually do that. Just throw it all out. Then go through and decide what you don't need or wear and donate it. Put everything else back into the closet in an organized manner.

Take one out each time you put a new one in

Each time that you go to the store and purchase a new item, you need to take an item out of the closet. If you continue to add more things to your closet without ever cleaning it out, you are quickly going to end up with a big mess in there again. You can take an item out and throw it away or donate it, but never add in a new item without clearing out an old one first. This helps you to keep your closet clean.

Assess the obstacles that are the biggest

Take a look inside your closet and determine what is going to be the biggest obstacle for you to handle. Do you see that you have a ton of shoes that are taking over everything? Go through them and decide which ones you want to keep, and which ones you can get rid of. Then get a hanging shoe rack or an over-the-door organizer to put them in. Do you see that the clothes in your closet are overcrowding everything else?

Get some thinner hangers (after clearing out the clothes you will never wear).

Another option you have is to organize the clothes in your closet based on what they are. For example, you can divide up the closet based on jeans, dresses, shirts, and so on, making it easier to find the things that you need. This can bring about some order in your closet, while also saving you some time when looking for an outfit in the morning.

Treat your wardrobe like it is a time capsule

Many times we hold onto clothes, shoes, and other items that we never use just because they hold a special meaning to us, or because we hope to someday be able to wear them. But that dress that you haven't worn since high school, or those skinny jeans that are still six sizes too small when you haven't eaten healthily or worked out in months is simply taking up room. It is time to go through and get rid of anything that isn't part of your signature look.

This signature look includes all the outfits that you wear on a regular basis. These are the clothes that make you look good, and the ones that make you feel comfortable, so you are more likely to wear them. Sure, that dress may look nice, and that suit outfit may seem really cool in the closet, but if they are just sitting there and never being used, then they are not worth your time.

Essentially, when you combine together all your articles of clothing, including shirts, dress clothes, pants, sweaters, and shoes, you should only have about 30 to 40 pieces. This is plenty to mix and match to get all the different styles and looks that you want. Anything that doesn't make the list should be donated or tossed out to clear up space in your closet.

Ask some questions that may be tough

When you are looking through the closet, you need to think through a lot of hard questions about each item you take out. Besides asking when was the last time that you wore a particular article of clothing, you should also ask some other questions including:

- Is this article a representation of my fantasy self or myself that I wish I could be? Or is it something that I would actually wear?

- Do I need to weigh a certain amount in order to feel good while wearing this article of clothing?

- Is the upkeep a pain for this article of clothing? Is it only dry clean, does it show wear and tear easily, or do you need to iron it before you can wear it again? Is the upkeep really worth your time?

- The last time that I put this article on, how did I feel?

If your answer on these questions is negative, then you may want to get rid of that item. If it is something that is bulky but you treasure it because it's an heirloom, or has a lot of sentimental value, then you can consider putting those items in storage somewhere to get them out of the way.

Don't consider the return on investment

Many people will hold onto an item because it cost them an arm and a leg and they want to get their money's worth out of that item. But instead of actually using that item, they will just stuff it back into the closet for another time, and encounter the same problem the next time they try to declutter. If you are looking for the return on investment with all the items in your closet, you are going to be holding onto a lot of items that you shouldn't.

Sure, you may have spent a lot of money on that designer name bag or on those shoes, but if you never actually use those items, then it is just collecting dust and taking up space. Instead, learn from that mistake and don't make it again in the future, and then donate that item or give it away to someone who may actually get some use out of it.

Cleaning out the closet can be a big chore. A lot of things have gotten shoved in there throughout the time, and when you finally decide to go through it, the place can be a horrible mess. Figuring out what you should get rid of and what you should keep can be a hassle. But following the steps above can really help make it easier to complete.

Chapter 15:
Daily Tips to Make
Decluttering Your Life
Easier

Decluttering your life doesn't have to be difficult, even though it may take some time depending on how messy your home is. The hardest part is coming up with a plan and getting started so that you can start seeing the results. Some of the tips that you can follow when it is time to start decluttering your home includes:

Engage others to help out around the house

Decluttering the home and keeping it looking nice does not have to be just your job. Many times, only one person is doing all the work, and this can get exhausting. If you are constantly picking up and decluttering everything in the home, you can feel resentful and may be more likely to give up because nothing ever seems to get done. A better approach is to get everyone in your home involved in the process.

There are a ton of benefits to doing things this way. First, it takes some of the work off your shoulders. Instead of you having to go through every room in the house and declutter and instead of only you having to make sure the house stays decluttered, you can get everyone on board with the idea to help.

This can include your husband, your kids if they are old enough, and everyone else. When you share the work, it doesn't seem as bad to handle and you won't feel you are fighting an uphill battle. Lastly, everyone in the home will start to appreciate the effort that it takes, and how nice the home feels when the decluttering process is done.

Do the dishes once you are done cooking or after a meal

No one likes to do the dishes. There is just something about them that can make everyone annoyed, and many quickly run to find something else to get done instead. And it doesn't help that those dishes need to be taken care of a few times a day, or they seem to pile up. Many of us put off doing dishes until the end of the night, or even wait a few days before touching the dishes, simply because we don't like to do them. Then, by the time we get to them, they have lots of stuck on food particles, the piles are high, and the work has multiplied.

One thing that you can do to help keep your kitchen looking nice and organized, is to just do the dishes when a meal is done. This will only include a few dishes at a time, unless you really had a messy prep for the meal, and can ensure that the kitchen always looks nice and clean. It may seem like a big hassle, but having all the dishes put away and looking nice can go a long way in helping declutter that kitchen of yours.

In addition to taking some time to clean the dishes after you are done with the meal, spend a few minutes tidying up the rest of the kitchen, and even the rest of the home. If you have done well with maintaining the decluttering since you did the main process, and you have gotten everyone else on board to help you out, you can spend ten to fifteen minutes each night maintaining the cleanliness, before you can sit down and relax for the night with a clean home.

If you have some time, and a little bit of ambition, take this time to prepare yourself for the next day. For example, you can easily set out your keys, the clothes you want to wear the next day, the homework for your kids, and anything else that you need to take to work with you the following day. Most people don't need a ton of items to help them get started for the next day, but it is always easier to do it right away at night, rather than scrambling around in the morning when you are tired.

Listen to some music when you clean up

Nothing motivates quite as well as some good music. If you have a lot of decluttering to get done, or you need to get a lot of cleaning done in a short amount of time, then turn on the radio or your own music player and get to work right away.

Studies have shown how positive and upbeat music can make all the difference when it comes to how much work you can get done. It can help you to focus on the task at hand, it can set the speed at which you clean, and it can even help you to be in a better mood while decluttering. You can be the one who chooses the type of music, but something that helps you be upbeat and stay focused on the task at hand can make a big difference.

Set a timer to get the tasks done

Many of us like to procrastinate when it comes to getting tasks done. We think it is going to take forever to finish, and we just don't want to put in the time to make it happen. Instead of getting started with the work and just getting it done, we keep putting it off, only doing a little bit at a time, and other tasks that make it very hard to ever get anything done. We end up with a self-fulfilling prophecy of the task actually taking as long as we feared.

If we just got on top of that task right away, rather than messing around, things wouldn't be so bad. And this is where the timer can come in to help. When you are ready to do a task, set your timer and then get to work. Set it for fifteen to twenty minutes (most tasks won't take longer than this if you really get to work), and then spend that time just focusing on that task. You may even be able to get the task done faster, then move on to another one and see what you can get done in that time.

Often our fear of getting started on a new task is because we are worried that it will take too long. But most of the tasks that we need to complete don't take as long as you think they will. Just set that timer and don't focus on anything else until it is done.

Don't rely on storage units

One trap that a lot of people will fall into when they are decluttering their lives, is the idea that they can just move their items to storage units. They will go through a lot of the topics that we discussed in this guidebook, and then add in another pile; a pile that allows them to move their unused items to a storage unit. All this does is move the clutter to another area, rather than letting you deal with it.

If you choose to rely on a storage unit, you are just making the process worse. It is easy to grab some items and move it to the storage unit, knowing that it is still there if you need it. You aren't learning how to get rid of items that you don't need for good, then you will continue to purchase more items, and keep going through the same process that got you in this mess to start with.

In addition to still keeping around the clutter, even though it is moved to a new location, you are adding another bill to your month. Now, you not only pay the mortgage on your home, but you are also spending money to maintain an area that just holds onto your junk and clutter. This is a horrible way to waste money just to make decluttering easier when it actually makes the process more difficult.

If you want to take an item and place it in storage, then that is probably a good sign that you should just get rid of the item. Most of the time, when you put something in the storage unit, you will completely forget about it. They will keep paying the storage unit fee each month, and then never see those items for two, three, or more years. This is just a waste of your time and money. It is much better for you to take that item and donate it, or throw it away. You aren't going to use that item anyway, so you may as well throw it out rather than spending money on a storage unit that holds your trash.

Plan out what you need to do tomorrow

Each night before you head to bed, take some time to make plans for the next day. When we wake up in the morning, we are often tired and worn out. We are trying to get up and get some things done. We are trying to get out the door for work, and school, and everything else. It is hard to get our minds to work and remember all the things that need to be done.

This is why you should make a plan the night before and write it down. Find everything important that you need right away in the morning, get the coffee pot ready to go, and lay out the clothes for the kids. Write down everything that you need to get done in the morning before you even head off to work. If there is something important that you need to get done at some other time of the day, write that information down as well.

This process only has to take about five minutes at night, but it can really help make your day better. It keeps you more organized, helps you to stay on track, and prevents some of the big issues that can come up when you spend most of your morning searching around for your keys or other items.

Chapter 16:
Different Techniques You Can Use to Make Decluttering a Breeze

T he topic of decluttering is a large one, and because of this, many people have come up with their own techniques to make decluttering easier than ever. There are actually many methods that you can use to help declutter your home, your mind, and everything else in your life. Let's take a look at some of the best methods that you can choose when you are worried about getting started with decluttering.

KonMarie Method

This is a method that was made popular by Marie Kondo, and it is actually one of the most popular and a well-known method for decluttering that is out there. The core idea behind this method is that instead of deciding what you want to get rid of when you clean your home, you will instead choose what you would like to keep, and then declutter the rest.

To start out with this method, you will collect every item that you own that fits in a particular category and then add it to one large pile. For example, you may be working on clothes at this time so you would go and collect every t-shirt that you own and lay them out on the bed. Then take each one and hold it, feel it, or wear it to help you get a sense of how it makes you feel.

While you are wearing that item, ask if it brings a spark of joy to your heart or not? Depending on how you feel about that item, you will decide whether or not to keep that item and then move on to the next. You can do this with every item that you own if you want.

The positives of the KonMarie method are that it is very thorough, and it allows you to compare all the items that you have that are similar. This helps you to easily get rid of any duplicates that are out there, and you can easily compare items that you don't like as much or that are well-worn, to newer and better item, resulting in an easy way to get rid of some of the old. It is a very effective way to make progress when you are trying to declutter specific categories that have been spread around the house.

However, this method can be very time-consuming and will mean that you need to sort through a whole bunch of stuff in this manner. Instead of focusing on just doing one room or two rooms at a time, you are going through and pulling out things from the whole house, and this could cause quite a mess when you try to clean up.

The Minimalist Game

This is a method that is going to take the experience that comes with decluttering and turns it into a game. It is a popular method of decluttering where hundreds of people will use their #minsgame hashtag on social media each month.

The basics of this game is that on the first day of the month, the number of things that you are going to declutter will correspond with the day of the month. So, on the first day of the month, you will declutter one item, on the second day, you get rid of two items, and so on. By the time you get to the end of the month, you will remove 496 items from the home if you make it all the way through. This becomes even more fun if you can challenge a friend or a family member to see who can keep going with this for the longest.

One benefit of doing this is that when the month is done, if you keep up with it, you will have gotten rid of a ton of stuff. Removing 300 items from your home is a big task, and you can play for as many months as you would like. It helps that you start out small and then increase the amount over time. This can be nice for those who are looking to build up their confidence in their decision-making abilities, and you will get better at letting stuff go.

There are some negatives that come with this method. A major issue with it is that you need to stay consistent with this or you are going to fall behind. Much like Tetris, the difficult is going to increase each level and it can be difficult to keep up once you fall behind. And when you reach the end of the month, you may find that it is a bit overwhelming to find 20 some items to get rid of when you are tired from work.

The Four Box Method

Another method that you may want to try out is one that is known as the four box method. This is a flexible method that can help you deal with all the items that are cluttering up your home. You can do it for however long you want and the frequency you prefer. By sorting the clutter into four categories, you are going to make a decision for every item that is out of place in your home.

The basic with this method is that you will go into a room and label four boxes. These can be labeled as put away, give away, undecided, and throw away. Then you will go through the room and pick up the clutter that is there and place it in one of those four boxes. Every item needs to go into one of those boxes. The undecided box is a nice addition because you can put stuff in there that you are not sure about, but if you want to have a plan for everything, then get rid of this one box.

The positive of working with this method of decluttering is that it is pretty easy to understand, and there is a category available for everything. The items that go in the undecided box are ones that you will reconsider later at some other time. This gives you a lot of flexibility and lets you declutter the room at the pace that works the best for you.

The issue with this method is that if you are not careful, that undecided box can become a big problem as more things start to pile up inside it. If you are worried about misusing this box, consider going down to three boxes so you will actually make a decision about all the items.

One Method

If you like the ideas that come with a few of these methods, then the one method is the best for you. This method was created by taking similar philosophies and combining them together into one concept that is easy to understand. The idea behind this one is that you will get rid of just one thing every day for a set period of time. You can pick out how long you want to do this for. Many start with a month and then move from there. The one thing that you get rid of can be one item, one box that is filled, one filled up bag, or anything else that works the best for you.

The benefit of the One Method is that it can help you to build up a habit of decluttering without taking too much effort. Since you just have to get rid of one thing every day, you are learning how to build decluttering into your daily routine, so all that clutter doesn't end up coming back and being in the way. Another benefit that comes with this method is that you can create your own system, and you can choose how much you want to get rid of (single item versus a box full) depending on your activity level, and how much you need to get all cleaned up.

Due to the consistency that is required for this method and for some people with a busy schedule, it can be hard to keep up with. Or if there are times when you need to be away from home, this is going to be difficult to keep up as well. This method wouldn't work well for those who want to do the work in a big burst, rather than little steps either.

Packing Party

Another method that you can try out is a fairly common method, and it is one that you are already using if you plan to move into a new location. While it does take some preparation to make it work, and you may need to enlist some help from friends, it can be effective if you can make it through.

The basics of this one is you will have some people come over, and pack everything that you own into boxes as if you are about to move. Then, through the next few months or so, only take out the items that you actually use. After three months have passed, any item that is left in the box needs to be donated or sold because you aren't likely to use it.

One of the benefits of this method is that it can definitely help you get rid of the items that you don't use. Things that are out of sight can often be out of mind, and you may not miss a lot of the items that are in the box. It can take some time to accomplish, but it ensures that you are getting rid of everything that you no longer needs.

The negative of this method is that it may not make a ton of sense unless you are already in the process of packing up to move. Not only does it take up a ton of energy and time, you already have to go out searching for, or purchasing boxes to make this happen. And it may not work well if you have some seasonal items or items that you only take out a few times a year anyway.

The Closet Hanger Method

The final method that we are going to talk about is one that helps you figure out what items in the home you actually use. This method allows you to track exactly what has been used in your home, without having to go through such massive methods like the packing party.

As the name suggests, you are going to work on cleaning out your closet, but you can adjust it to some other items as well. When you begin, turn all the hangers in the closet to face the same direction. As you war the items, you will put them back into the closet, but you will turn the hanger around the opposite direction to help show that you actually wore that item. Over time, you will be able to tell which items you actually wear, and which ones are just sitting in the closet and taking up space.

This type of decluttering method is really easy to implement and doesn't take you a ton of time to get started with. It is a clear-cut way to see just what you are using out of your closet and what you don't use. This method works the best for helping you to clean out your closet, and get rid of the clothes that you no longer wear, but you can certainly adjust it to help you declutter other items throughout your home.

Since this method is specifically designed to help with clothing, it can be difficult depending on what other items you want to get rid of. Plus, if you have any items that need to be folded and put in your dresser, this method won't work as well. You need to have some discipline to make sure that the clothing item gets put back into your closet, and facing the right way after you wear it, or this method is not going to work.

For items that aren't considered clothing and can't be hung up, this method can be hard to work with and you may not be sure what method to use, or what variation to use, to make it work. This is another method that doesn't work well with items that are for special occasions, or for any of the seasonal items that you own.

These are some of the most popular decluttering methods that you can choose to implement into your cleaning process. All of these can be implemented to give you some great results with how clean your home can be, and can be used with the different strategies that we talked about before. Take a look at some of these methods, and decide which one will work the best for your particular cleaning style and for decluttering your home.

Conclusion

Decluttering your home, as well as other parts of your life can really make a difference. You are going to feel less stressed out. You can spend less time worrying about cleaning the house, and more time doing the things that you love. You can actually take up a hobby, spend time with friends and family, and just enjoy life.

Our modern society has put too much emphasis on owning material possessions. We think that we will be able to find happiness with material things. And the advertisements that we see around us all the time do nothing to help with this issue. Many people have started to assign feelings and value to items that shouldn't be there, and this makes it very easy to collect more, and hard to let these things go.

Decluttering and minimalism work against this idea. While you don't have to get rid of everything in your home to follow these ideas, it is important to realize what can stay and what needs to go. Holding onto things just because you think they are valuable, or because you give them extra value in your head that shouldn't be there, and we refuse to let items go when they are just in the way. With decluttering, it is time to let go of these things, and learn which items to keep that actually bring us some happiness.

This guidebook took some time to talk about decluttering and why it is such an important process to work on. We took a look at some of the basics that come with decluttering, what the minimalist lifestyle is like and why it can be so beneficial, some of the top reasons that people refuse to get started with decluttering their own lives, and so much more.

We then moved on to some of the steps that you can take to declutter every room in your home. Remember, you only need to work on one room at a time and only for an hour or so at a time. If you get overwhelmed, or you have a busy schedule and need to take a bit longer, then that is fine. This is the beauty of working with decluttering, as long as you make progress forward, and don't start reintroducing more stuff back into the home at the same time, then you are doing it the right way.

This guidebook ends with some tips to make the decluttering process easier, along with a discussion about which methods are popular, and how you can get each one to work. All of the methods can work, you just need to pick out the one that you can stick with, the one that will work the best for you and your style of cleaning out the clutter.

When you are ready to make some changes in your life, and finally get rid of all the stuff that is in your home, all the stuff that you constantly need to clean up and that is always in the way, all the stuff that takes up your time away from the people and things you really love, then this guidebook is for you. It will show you all the steps you need to take to finally get rid of that clutter for good.

About the Author

Mary Connor is a professional organizer, a wife and mom to three children, a cleaning expert, and a former finance manager. She is passionate about helping people lead better lives and shares easy and inexpensive organizing tips and tricks on how to clean up life's little and big messes. In addition, she teaches women how to pay off debts, improve their money management skills and increase their wealth.

In the past, Mary found her passion in writing and focuses on topics that can make a real difference in helping others accomplish their goals and dreams. She has made it a habit to continue learning new things so that she can share these insights with the world in a concise and helpful way. This interest has led her to the life of learning several factors affecting human interactions. Moreover, she continually works on expanding her knowledge by attending seminars and networking with other professionals.

Mary loves the outdoors and likes to walk or run every day. She is dedicated to the practice of mindfulness and feels that a minimalist lifestyle is important to both success and happiness. When not writing or walking, Mary enjoys spending time horseback riding with her daughters or relaxing at the lake with her husband.